Especially for

....

From

....

Date

....

A Devotional Journal

When *Jesus* Speaks
to a
Mother's Heart

Shelley R. Lee

BARBOUR BOOKS
An Imprint of Barbour Publishing, Inc.

I AM

*Jesus said to them, "Truly, truly, I say to you,
before Abraham was born, I am."*
JOHN 8:58 NASB

Yes, I said these words when I walked the earth, and it really stirred things up! People weren't expecting a common man like Me; they were looking for a kingly type. And, well, you likely know that I am the King, but this seemed blasphemous to many of them at the time.

My Father, the Holy Spirit, and I make up the triune God. We are One. I was there at creation and all along with My Father. I know it can be hard for the human mind to grasp, but the Holy Spirit will help you begin to wrap your mind around this and many other things.

As a mother you are especially in need of His guidance. You know that so much is riding on how you parent your precious children. I don't need to tell you that. You love them inexplicably! I want you to know that I love them and you even more!

It's pretty impossible to comprehend the depth of My love, but parenting comes close. It's the closest look you'll get this side of heaven, and I want to help you do your very best—beyond your best, actually. Because I am the One who can fill any gaps you may have in parenting.

*God, how I need You in my giant job as a mother.
Help me to listen to Your Word and Your guidance. Amen.*

THE REAL ENEMY

For we do not wrestle against flesh and blood, but against the rulers, against the authorities, against the cosmic powers over this present darkness, against the spiritual forces of evil in the heavenly places.
EPHESIANS 6:12 ESV

There are many dark things woven into your life on different levels, many that you don't even recognize yet. Let Me encourage you with important truth right where you are.

Remember that the battle is spiritual. No matter how much it may seem at times that people are against you, the root of all trouble and opposition to what is good and true is always the Enemy of your soul. He seeks to destroy you and your children in any way he can.

Be super alert, like a neighborhood watch over your heart and over everything that regards your children. Never forget, I am the all-powerful Victor! No matter how overwhelmed you may feel, keep in mind that I am far bigger.

Pray. Talk to My Father and Me frequently (Ephesians 6:18 MSG) about whatever you are facing or fearing. There is tremendous power in prayer. You are so dear to Me, My Father, and the Holy Spirit. We've got your back!

Father God, my family and I are depending on You today. Thank You for being my Protector, Defender, and Warrior in the raging spiritual battles that I am oft unaware of. You are so good to me! Amen.

HOPE FOR TODAY

*I would have despaired unless I had believed that I would see
the goodness of the L*ORD *in the land of the living. Wait for the L*ORD;
*be strong and let your heart take courage; yes, wait for the L*ORD.*
PSALM 27:13–14 NASB

My dear child, I know the things that cause you to despair in this
earthly life—deeply, at times.

You know you have the promise of eternal life without decay or death
of any kind, but I want to give you hope for right now, too. I will show My
goodness to you and your children in this life, today. I will not wait for
eternity to bless you—of that you can be sure! Be patient.

This day, be strong in what you know. Be brave and do the right
things. Remember, these are much simpler than many people think,
like responding lovingly to your child when he makes a mistake or comforting
him when he's afraid. Care for your child physically and spiritually in
every small way you can think of today.

My goodness is going to come to you.

*Lord God, thank You for the hope You give me for this
day and each day into eternity. Strengthen me to be all
I can for You and for my children today. Amen.*

HEAVY LIFTING

"Come to me, all who labor and are heavy laden, and I will give you rest. Take my yoke upon you, and learn from me, for I am gentle and lowly in heart, and you will find rest for your souls. For my yoke is easy, and my burden is light."
MATTHEW 11:28–30 ESV

Your burdens for your children are tremendous at times, and rightly so. Their lives are precious, and you have a weighty job being their mother!

It may sound cliché, but I really do want to take your burdens.

You have so much to juggle; I watch you. You care for your little ones and do so many things at the same time. You'll have laundry going while dinner is cooking. Meanwhile, you'll get a Band-Aid for one and water for another, pick up toys, settle an argument, set the table, and update the family calendar. All the while, there are bigger burdens than daily, routine things—the ones that feel like a lead vest. The good news is that I want to lighten all of this for you. Hand over all of it; let Me do all I know you need help with. I'll give you a light load that you can walk with through the day and feel good about.

Lord, help me to give over my burdens to You.
Provide the relief and rest I need to be the best I can
be for the children You've entrusted to me. Amen.

LIMITLESS LOVE

For I am convinced that neither death, nor life, nor angels, nor principalities, nor things present, nor things to come, nor powers, nor height, nor depth, nor any other created thing, will be able to separate us from the love of God, which is in Christ Jesus our Lord.
ROMANS 8:38–39 NASB

If I could articulate this in person to you right now, I would shout from the top of the nearest hilltop where you and a lot of other people could hear Me loud and clear, "I *love* this woman! I *love* her!" And of course I would be pointing at you the whole time.

I am not sure you realize that there isn't a single thing you can do that could keep Me from loving you like this. No behavior, no attitude, no bad decision. No evil act by another, no loss, no hidden past. Nothing.

No poor judgment as a mother. No yelling rant. No abandonment. There is literally nothing you have done, do, or will do that will keep Me from loving you.

I love you, and I always will. My love changes your life. It makes you the mother you want to be, the person you want to be.

I love you!

Lord, help me remember Your eternal, undying love for me, that I may grow in it and shine Your love on my children. Amen.

GROW YOUR PASSION

For where jealousy and selfish ambition exist, there is disorder and every
evil thing. But the wisdom from above is first pure, then peaceable, gentle,
reasonable, full of mercy and good fruits, unwavering, without hypocrisy.
JAMES 3:16–17 NASB

When you are tempted to be jealous of someone else's abilities and circumstances, I want you to remember something. You have been made with a special set of abilities and attributes that are fitted for a wonderful purpose in the life where you are, as well as where you are going!

You may think this is just something Christians say to feel better about their place in life, but I'm very serious about this. Looking at other mothers who you perceive have a better life or skill set than yours will lead to many false thoughts and ideas. It will hinder your relationships and your self-image.

You know what you love, where your passion is. I will give you the wisdom to grow in your strengths. So keep asking Me, and keep growing. You are a beautiful mother, and you're growing more beautiful all the time.

Dear Lord, thank You for the strengths You have given me.
Show me how to grow in them, that I may serve You
exceedingly well. Amen.

KEEP LOOKING UP

A cheerful disposition is good for your health;
gloom and doom leave you bone-tired.
PROVERBS 17:22 MSG

Life is full of challenges as a mother, and you can be sure that I see them all. Thankfully there are many wonderful things, too, and even when it doesn't feel like it, they outweigh the tough ones. Your children are gifts as well as all that is provided for you to care for them. On top of that, there is the beauty of creation that is everywhere. Check it out!

If you keep looking at the positive things and keep your focus there, you will have a better outlook on life. As a side effect, the toxic energy produced by negativity will be absent from your body and will you have better health.

I'm not saying you shouldn't acknowledge the hard things in life; of course not! You must face difficulties to move through them. You will definitely walk through very low spots on your way to better places; the key is to not hang out there. No camping in the valley, that's the idea.

Keep looking up, and concentrate on what is good. I'm leading you to great places!

Lord, thank You for all that is good in this day and in my life.
You have blessed me. Help me to count the many ways! Amen.

THE GREATEST WORK OF ALL

*But my life is worth nothing to me unless I use it for finishing
the work assigned me by the Lord Jesus—the work of telling
others the Good News about the wonderful grace of God.*
ACTS 20:24 NLT

The work you have as a mother sharing the Gospel of grace with
your children is powerfully and eternally significant. You have the
opportunity to change their lives here on earth and forever!

Remember this—your work is vital. Don't underestimate or short-sell
the potential impact of simply sharing and shining My love every day.

Each opportunity you have to show grace and teach mercy, do it. Tell
them all about Me. How I died that they might have life. How I am with
them always. How they can know Me personally, just like you. You will be
surprised how much their young hearts understand.

Keep growing and glowing in My love. The effect your family can have
on those around you will be amazing. It is something I love to see!

◇◇

*Dear God, give me the grace and strength I need to extend the same
grace You offer me to my children, that they may know You. Amen.*

HINDRANCES

*Therefore, since we are surrounded by such a huge crowd of
witnesses to the life of faith, let us strip off every weight that slows
us down, especially the sin that so easily trips us up. And let us
run with endurance the race God has set before us.*
HEBREWS 12:1 NLT

What is it that weighs you down in your faith walk? What keeps you from being the best mother you can be?

I can see what it is, but you have to see it for yourself for it to make a difference for you.

Look to Me; I can help you see clearly, and I can help you clear away the roadblocks in your path.

So tell Me what you see that is hindering you. Is there unforgiveness? Unrealistic expectations? Are there lies you need truth to dispel? Is there a sin habit that is entangling you? Whatever it is, remember that I want to help you with this.

There's a great run ahead for you!

*Lord God, give me eyes to see the hindrances in my way,
and then help me to lay them aside. These things are
way too big for me. I need Your help. Amen.*

SWIFT GRACE

Be angry, and yet do not sin; do not let the sun go down on
your anger, and do not give the devil an opportunity.
EPHESIANS 4:26–27 NASB

There are things in the day to day as a mother that can get you very upset. Sometimes it's your children who have done things; other times it's other children, or worse—their parents (they are human, just like you!). Try to remember that handling anger is nothing new, and you can get through it without losing control. I promise.

Though you may tremble with emotion at times, don't let it get ahold of you. Forgive swiftly rather than holding a grudge. If it's your children, discipline fairly and help them see you still love them no matter what. Learning and practicing to forgive others quickly, the way I forgive you, is a wonderful exercise that will make you stronger.

Before you go to sleep each night, talk to Me. I can help you see who you need to forgive so your heart isn't darkened in any way.

Lord, bring to mind for me those I've held things
against, and help me to forgive them. You are the
Master of forgiveness. Show me the way. Amen.

THE PEACE RULE

And let the peace of Christ rule in your hearts, to which
indeed you were called in one body. And be thankful.
COLOSSIANS 3:15 ESV

So much that is unsettling can settle in around you. In the midst of it all, I want you to know that the peace I give to you can empower you entirely. My peace can reign beautifully over your heart.

You can face everything that weaves its way into your world today, not only as a mother but in every role in the unique life that is yours.

When just a hint of unrest threatens to disrupt you, remember to lean into Me. Trust Me. This peace that I'll give you is an indescribable steadiness that you can get nowhere else. Not anywhere!

I made this world, and I know how to help you through it, even now in its fallen state.

I've watched you try to find peace by worldly means, but you know now how it just doesn't work. I long to bless you in many ways, and I will, but real peace can only be found in Me. I offer it to you now and always.

Lord God, let Your sovereign peace fill my heart and
my entire presence today. I need You every minute
in this complex life, Lord. I need You! Amen.

TRUTH STOREHOUSE

Let the word of Christ dwell in you richly, teaching and admonishing
one another in all wisdom, singing psalms and hymns and
spiritual songs, with thankfulness in your hearts to God.
COLOSSIANS 3:16 ESV

There will be times when you are incapacitated. You've already experienced some of them, like when you gave birth to your child or when you have been ill. During these stretches of time, you may not be able to be in My Word like you want to or should.

I want you to keep storing up My Word in your heart and mind. Let it fill every empty space you can manage. Not only will this help you when you are at full-functioning capacity as a mother and in every other role, but when you enter these times of incapacity, you will also have a reserve of truth and spiritual food to keep going. I will always provide for you and strengthen you when you need it, but if you do this, you are more likely to be able to minister to your children and others around you in a time of weakness for yourself.

So do it! Store up My Word; it's a treasure. Then just wait and see what I will do!

Lord, bless this day with Your truth that will remain in
my heart. Help me to remember it when it is needed to
help me or someone else You put in my path. Amen.

FINISHING WHAT WE STARTED

*And I am sure of this, that he who began a good work
in you will bring it to completion at the day of Jesus Christ.*
PHILIPPIANS 1:6 ESV

We started something with you, My Father, the Holy Spirit, and I. You didn't see the beginning of it, but I did, and the whole thing is so beautiful! First, let Me go back a ways. We created you, and wow, We were so excited about the gifts We gave you and how wonderfully you were made! Then the Holy Spirit started to move in your midst and in your heart. I loved watching the whole process.

The great thing is that the work in you just keeps going.

So when you are discouraged about how things are going with your big assignment as a mother, remember this: I am committed to completing the work I started in you. You can count on it!

What's more, I am doing the same thing for your children. The work just keeps on going. So be encouraged; I am not done yet!

*God, thank You for the work You continue to do in me
and in my children. I am grateful for Your faithfulness to me.
Help me to be faithful in return to serve You well. Amen.*

GUARD THE DOOR

*For though we walk in the flesh, we are not waging war
according to the flesh. For the weapons of our warfare are not
of the flesh but have divine power to destroy strongholds. We destroy
arguments and every lofty opinion raised against the knowledge
of God, and take every thought captive to obey Christ.*
2 CORINTHIANS 10:3–5 ESV

You feel the things that come against you and your children. You know they are there, but things can get dark and confusing very quickly, and you may at times feel powerless against the Enemy of your soul.

I want you to know that you have divine power through Me. With spiritual alertness and prayer, so much can be defended and conquered. Start at the door of your mind. Whenever an untrue or doubtful thought tries to get in, bring it to Me. I will help you sort it out, and this way you can get rid of lies and deceit before they grow in your mind with other thoughts.

The Enemy works in subtle ways, so be watchful and prayerful. Remember where your power comes from and that I am with you always!

*Lord God, give me discernment today over my thought
life. Bring truth to the forefront, that my children
and I will not be deceived by the Enemy. Amen.*

REMEMBER

*The lines have fallen to me in pleasant places; indeed,
my heritage is beautiful to me. I will bless the LORD who has
counseled me; indeed, my mind instructs me in the night.
I have set the LORD continually before me; because
He is at my right hand, I will not be shaken.*

PSALM 16:6–8 NASB

Where I have placed you is no accident! Many have come before you in both your natural and your faith families, and you are right where you should be in all of it. I get very excited thinking about the impact you can have as a mother and in all the circles you are a part of!

I want you to celebrate the good moments and live with thanksgiving in those days. I love to bless you.

There are times when I know things can get really complicated, when it all feels like a big wreck. Try to remember it's a beautiful collision that I am going to do something spectacular with. I promise.

In all that happens with you and your children, the goodness that came before you and that is coming abounds with magnificence. I wish I could give you a mental download of it all, but little by little is best. Just remember.

*Dear God, thank You for the beauty of Your master plan and
that You have a special place for me in it all. Strengthen
me for the piece of it that will unfold today. Amen.*

DEPENDABLE HELPER

*No test or temptation that comes your way is beyond the
course of what others have had to face. All you need to remember
is that God will never let you down; he'll never let you be pushed past
your limit; he'll always be there to help you come through it.*

1 CORINTHIANS 10:13 MSG

When your children push all your buttons and the people you care about the most let you down—these are just two instances when you are tempted to turn the wrong way. But I will help you through every tempting, testy time you experience.

You may feel like you will break under the pressure, for it can be great, but it will never be greater than your limit—because I am with you!

The Enemy will want you to feel guilty for just being tempted, but I want you to know if you keep seeking My help in these times, you have no guilt. You have victory! Stay with Me; I'll see you through.

*Lord, give me a knee-jerk reaction, whenever I am tempted,
to turn immediately to You for help. I need You, Lord, so I don't
fall into the many temptations that come my way. Amen.*

KEEP ON PRAYING

*This is the confidence which we have before Him, that,
if we ask anything according to His will, He hears us. And if we
know that He hears us in whatever we ask, we know that
we have the requests which we have asked from Him.*
1 JOHN 5:14–15 NASB

know there are things you have asked for and have received a big fat "no" or "not now" as an answer. That's hard. I know.

I want to encourage you! My Father knows exactly what you need and what is the very best for you. He will not do anything that is not going to be in your best interest, and not just for right now either. He has all of eternity in mind for you, and your children, too.

Don't let this stop you from going to Him with your requests—not one bit! Keep up the prayers! He hears every single one—you can be sure of that. Each utterance on behalf of your children, whether spoken or thought, yelled or whispered. Every request cried out in tears, and in joy, too.

Just trust that He will give you and your kids the absolute best. He will.

*Dear God, even when I don't understand the whys of
unanswered prayers, help me to trust You entirely. Amen.*

KEEP ON KEEPIN' ON

*Let us not become weary in doing good, for at the proper
time we will reap a harvest if we do not give up.*
GALATIANS 6:9 NIV

Tired? I see how worn out you can become, and I want to cheer you on! You can do this.

You get dog tired sometimes, doing all the right things in hundreds of ways every day for your children and those you love. I see that. There is joy in it for you, but it can all get absolutely exhausting. I see that, too!

I will strengthen you; just ask Me. But I want you to take the rest you need, care for yourself well, and keep on going in your good fight. It may be hard to believe, but amazing, miraculous things are going to come of your efforts, just you wait and see! The blessings of your tenacious labor on behalf of your children, especially, will be beyond what you can possibly imagine right now. Trust in Me. It is going to be spectacular!

*Lord God, I need You to give me the strength to keep going in what is
good and true. I have so much to do and so many demands.
Thank You that You know them all. Give me all
that I need today. Amen.*

A MILLION CHANCES TO SHOW GRACE

Use your heads as you live and work among outsiders.
Don't miss a trick. Make the most of every opportunity. Be gracious
in your speech. The goal is to bring out the best in others
in a conversation, not put them down, not cut them out.
COLOSSIANS 4:5–6 MSG

When you interact with those who don't know Me, I want you to be wise, gracious, and loving. Remember that I love every single person you bump into, whether it's your neighbor or your child's friend, that friend's family member, or maybe your child himself who needs Me. Reflect My love for them.

I will give you many opportunities to do this. Affirm the good in each person whenever you have the chance. Don't make them feel like your project; just enjoy them like you do your good friends. Include them in your life so that they can see the blessings of living a life of faith. But remember, just be gracious and kind. You'll notice that I repeated Myself. I'm glad you noticed! Be gracious.

Lord, fill me with Your grace today, that I may be a mirror of it
for others I encounter. I want to shine for You, God! Amen.

MAKING IT MATTER

*Yet you do not know what your life will be like tomorrow.
You are just a vapor that appears for a little while and then
vanishes away. Instead, you ought to say, "If the Lord
wills, we will live and also do this or that."*

JAMES 4:14–15 NASB

Y ou know that eternity with Me is a sealed deal if you indeed know Me
as your Savior. But there are no guarantees from one day to the next
in this earthly life for you or your children. It's all very fragile, and that's
easy to forget in the busyness of it all, isn't it?

With that in mind, make this day count for all you can. Do what you can
with all that you have been given, and know that whatever happens, I am
with you in it. Nothing surprises Me either, by the way! Keep looking up.
Between My Father, the Holy Spirit, and Me, you know the triune God has
you covered.

No matter how long the lives of you and your children are, they are
short in the scope of eternity—and at the same time, eternally significant
and precious.

*Lord God, give me eternal perspective in this day that is
but a breath. I need You to make it matter. Amen.*

MIRACULOUS MYSTERIES

But as for me, I will hope continually, and will praise You yet more and more. My mouth shall tell of Your righteousness and of Your salvation all day long; for I do not know the sum of them.
PSALM 71:14–15 NASB

Since I have been fully man, I know the limitations of understanding God from your perspective. It's. . .well, impossible really! It can be relatively easy to thank and praise God and Me for My sacrifice that brought salvation, but the mysteries of it are immense.

On the subject of Our righteousness, you can get the concept that God is perfect and fallen man needed My sacrifice to make friendship with God possible. But I'm telling you, My Father is so magnificently righteous it would blow you away!

And while you can see many of the things We are doing on behalf of you and your children, there is so much that is being done that you cannot see. It's beyond comprehension in the earthly state you are in. All you need to know is that amazing things are being accomplished in My Father's master plan, and you are a benefactor of all of it!

Lord, thank You for all You have done and are doing for me and my children. I can only begin to count it all. I rest in the mystery of Your miraculous work in the life of my family today. Amen.

SO MUCH GOOD TO THINK ON

Finally, brethren, whatever is true, whatever is honorable, whatever is right, whatever is pure, whatever is lovely, whatever is of good repute, if there is any excellence and if anything worthy of praise, dwell on these things.
PHILIPPIANS 4:8 NASB

With all the daily messes that make up motherhood, it can be hard to focus on what is good. If you are intentional though and look for the things that are right and true, I'm telling you, it will bless you!

You will begin to realize how much good there really is in the crazy world of mothering. Seriously!

There are people I have placed in your life who will make your day today. Some will be complete strangers. They will do one nice thing for you, and you will not see them again until eternity. Others are people who are your friends and neighbors who care for you. Of course there are your children who say the sweetest things and warm your heart. Write these down when you can and remember them.

There is beauty I have placed all around you. Stop. Look. It's all over the place in My vast creation. Enjoy it today!

Father God, thank You for all that is good in my life! Thank You for my children and all that You are doing for us. Amen.

WISE COUNSEL FOR MAMA

A wise man is strong, and a man of knowledge
increases power. For by wise guidance you will wage war,
and in abundance of counselors there is victory.
PROVERBS 24:5–6 NASB

R eal wisdom comes from God. You know, from My Father, the Holy
Spirit, and Me. You will need it as a mother. You know that, of course!
So ask for it often, and then you will be able to wisely apply your growing
knowledge.

Don't be afraid to ask for advice from others you have seen live wisely
in Me. In fact, ask a group of these people and you will have a wealth of
good thinking that will help you make better decisions.

People who neglect to seek advice and charge ahead with only their
thinking often lose out. They let their pride get in the way and miss many
victories because of it. You can do better. Wisdom and wise counsel await
you; go get them both, sweet woman whom I love!

Lord, give me wisdom for today, and show me those whom
I should seek counsel from as I seek to be the best mother
I can be for these children You have entrusted to me. Amen.

SOUL SWEETNESS

*Pleasant words are a honeycomb, sweet
to the soul and healing to the bones.*
PROVERBS 16:24 NASB

My words for you are profitable and forward moving. Try to let your words be this way, too, as much as you possibly can.

When you speak positively and lovingly, you speak life into others. Think of it—your children will grow under encouraging words just as flowers respond to water and sunshine. Upwardly getting stronger, they will send down healthy roots and display beautiful growth at the same time.

Even when delivering discipline to your children, you can speak with love and they will not question your heart for them. Every chance you get, offer words that are affirming and kind. You'll be surprised how fewer frowns there will be, how much anger is defused, how many low spirits are lifted, including yours! Before you know it, your sweet words will bring a blessing back to you in unexpected ways.

Even your health will benefit from speaking positive words. It affects all of you and those around you wonderfully!

*Lord God, help me speak life into those around me, including
myself, that I would reflect You as light and salt in the lives
of my children and all those I encounter today. Amen.*

STRENGTH IN HIS WORD

"Only be strong and very courageous; be careful to do according to all the law which Moses My servant commanded you; do not turn from it to the right or to the left, so that you may have success wherever you go. . .for then you will make your way prosperous, and then you will have success."

Joshua 1:7–8 nasb

What is it that you most need to be strong in today with mothering your children? I know the answer, but I want you to think about this for yourself.

There are many things you are learning and teaching your children every day. My Word will be a constant guide for you. Keep going with it, and find what you need so you can do your best for them. You will excel as a mother this way, I promise you!

Whether it is discipline or encouragement, grace or selflessness, perseverance or self-control, perhaps discernment or service, any or all of these your children may need to observe and absorb. Now, there's a challenge!

In Me you are strong every day. You can do this!

Lord, thank You for Your Word! Show me today exactly what I need to train my children in Your wisdom. Amen.

LEAN NOT ON YOURSELF

*Lean on, trust in, and be confident in the Lord with all your heart
and mind and do not rely on your own insight or understanding.
In all your ways know, recognize, and acknowledge Him,
and He will direct and make straight and plain your paths.*
PROVERBS 3:5–6 AMP

It may sound cliché, like the easy answer for how to best live—to trust Me with all your heart. But when it comes to your everyday living, you know just how hard it is!

You have been made with a great mind, so you can be quick to think you know what to do and that you know what's best. The Enemy will try to use all the great things My Father made against you by twisting things just right. So don't be fooled!

Trust Me in this great job of motherhood. Keep giving your heart over to Me, and when you need to make a decision, ask Me for direction. I'll give it to you every time.

In your thoughts, in your heart, with your words, and with your actions—just keep working at looking to Me first. You'll be amazed at how much better things will be for you and for your children.

*Dear God, thank You that I can trust You with my
heart! Give me the guidance I need this day to be the
mom I must be for these precious little ones. Amen.*

BETTER THAN CHRISTMAS MORNING

*For it is by free grace (God's unmerited favor) that you are saved
(delivered from judgment and made partakers of Christ's salvation) through
[your] faith. And this [salvation] is not of yourselves [of your own doing,
it came not through your own striving], but it is the gift of God.*
EPHESIANS 2:8 AMP

The greatest of all gifts: your salvation! I gladly sacrificed so this could be offered with no strings attached. Entirely free to you—I paid for it so you could be with Me in eternity.

It will be easy to forget that this gift comes with absolutely no ties to it. Because you want to serve Me and do the right things, you can easily fall into basing salvation on what you do. Make no such mistake.

For the sake of your children and those you love, make sure you tell them with all the grace you can that their actions do not determine their eternal destiny. Their relationship with Me does.

There's so much freedom in this attitude. You will stop judging others and yourself. You will live under grace and reflect grace. It's beautiful!

*Lord, help me to reflect Your grace today so my children
will eagerly accept the biggest and best gift of all: You! Amen.*

ANSWERS

"Thus says the LORD who made the earth, the LORD who formed it to establish it, the LORD is His name, 'Call to Me and I will answer you, and I will tell you great and mighty things, which you do not know.'"
JEREMIAH 33:2–3 NASB

I know there are countless questions you will want the answers to. Many of them will not be fully answered in this earthly life, but I want you to know that many can be!

I want to give you truth and help you uncover what you need to be the best person and most excellent mother you can be. So ask Me all the questions you want!

Then be prepared to listen. It can be hard to hear at times in the chaos of life, but something will come. As you know, sometimes the answer will simply be no. This can be very difficult to accept. I know.

At times the silence may seem cruel to you, but trust Me. The answers are often delivered in unexpected ways, but I promise—I will give you exactly what you need.

I love your questions and am endlessly creative. I have such great conversations about you with My Father and the Holy Spirit. There are wonderful things in store for you!

*Lord God, give me the answers I need for today,
and help me to trust You with every answer,
even when it's not what I thought
it should be. Amen.*

SO BLESSED

Behold, children are a gift of the LORD, the fruit of the womb is a reward. Like arrows in the hand of a warrior, so are the children of one's youth. How blessed is the man whose quiver is full of them.
PSALM 127:3–5 NASB

Your children are a blessing. I know you know that. But let's be honest, there are days when you wonder, aren't there? Days when things seem off kilter, when the timing of everything feels wrong. Days when your kids—well, let's just say it, they don't always *feel* like a blessing to you. You're human. They're human. It's not an easy road!

On these days, even if it's only for short moments, focus on the beauty of your children. Think on the sweet and funny things they say and do. Marvel at their innocence and curiosity—their incredible capacity for learning! Capture these moments any way you can, in writing or with photos. Admire your little ones while they're sleeping, and pray for the day ahead.

Remember that I love them even more than you do. That's hard to imagine, isn't it?

Lord, thank You for my children! Bless this day with beautiful moments that reflect Your goodness. Amen.

GOOD HABITS

All discipline for the moment seems not to be joyful, but sorrowful;
yet to those who have been trained by it, afterwards it yields
the peaceful fruit of righteousness. Therefore, strengthen the
hands that are weak and the knees that are feeble.
HEBREWS 12:11–12 NASB

The structure and boundaries you are giving your children have many layers. Some are simple physical things to keep them healthy and safe, while others will train them up for mental and spiritual growth.

It's all very important, of course. And all along, aren't you learning, too? I want you to know that I smile through this whole process. It is a beautiful thing!

Every bit of discipline that you teach and reinforce with care for your children will benefit them beyond their comprehension. But even you will be surprised by the results. So keep up the good work. Strengthen your children with healthy boundaries and daily practices that will help them become strong. In the process, you are getting stronger, too!

Lord God, thank You for Your guidance that allows me to guide
my children in the same ways. Give me the energy and wisdom
to provide all they need to be strong people
for Your glory. Amen.

ETERNAL IMPACT

*For momentary, light affliction is producing for us an eternal weight
of glory far beyond all comparison, while we look not at the things which
are seen, but at the things which are not seen; for the things which are
seen are temporal, but the things which are not seen are eternal.*
2 CORINTHIANS 4:17–18 NASB

In the many daily tasks that fill your time as a mother, you strive to do the best for your children each and every day. That is obvious. I see it.

Some of your trials are exhausting, and you may start to wonder why you have to endure so much, but I promise you—there is great reward for all of your efforts!

It can be hard to imagine beyond the things you see and walk through now in this earthly life. But I want to give you glimpses of eternity, the things you cannot see right now. What you are doing today, even the little things, it all makes an impact on eternity. The way you love your children ripples off to the way your whole family loves others. You are impacting so many in powerful ways.

It's mysterious, I know, but one day it will be crystal clear.

*Lord, give me the endurance to persevere. Help me
remember that You are making beauty from what can
feel ugly to me at times. I give You this day. Amen.*

JOY IN DREAMS

*Hope deferred makes the heart sick; but when
dreams come true at last, there is life and joy.*
PROVERBS 13:12 TLB

I want you to know that there is always hope! No matter what you are going through with your children, hope remains.

There are times when you need to see it to keep going. You can be sure that My Father will continue to give you a taste of your dreams and desires so that discouragement doesn't creep in and darken you.

I want to encourage you to do this in actions, too. You can work toward a desire of yours or help your children do this. It may be a small project that you really want to accomplish. Use the creativity you've been given, and do it! You will feel a lively satisfaction and give your kids a small picture of how God is working on things for you in much bigger ways.

My Father has given you dreams and desires for a reason. Keep seeking Our guidance, and keep growing. Watch patiently, and see how it all comes together.

◇◇◇◇◇◇◇◇◇◇◇◇◇◇◇◇◇◇◇◇◇◇◇◇◇◇◇◇◇◇◇◇◇◇

*Father God, I give You my desires today. I know not everything
I dream of may be realized in this earthly life, but I ask for Your hand
on the dreams I should pursue, that I would glorify You. Amen.*

FAITH IN THE CREATOR

Now faith is confidence in what we hope for and assurance about
what we do not see. This is what the ancients were commended for.
By faith we understand that the universe was formed at God's command,
so that what is seen was not made out of what was visible.

HEBREWS 11:1–3 NIV

You believe, even on the darkest days. You know that I am with you and that all I have promised is true. No matter the measure of your faith, it is so beautiful to Me!

You hear from the faithful that I will not forsake you and your children, that the great eternal promises will be fulfilled. Hang on to every bit of that Good News validated in My Word; it's absolutely true!

What I created (well, along with My Father and the Holy Spirit) is so incredibly vast that it's impossible for the human mind to begin to comprehend it. We spoke it all into being, and what a great time that was and still is! The best part was when We made you and your brothers and sisters in Our image. There are countless people, yet I know each and every one ever made or to be formed.

When you, My dear child, are counted among those with faith, I couldn't be more thrilled!

Lord, You are amazing! Thank You for giving me faith
in the unseen. I put my trust in You this day. Amen.

RENEWAL ABOUNDS

"Forget the former things; do not dwell on the past. See, I am doing a new thing! Now it springs up; do you not perceive it? I am making a way in the wilderness and streams in the wasteland."
ISAIAH 43:18–19 NIV

The Enemy of your soul likes to remind you of your past, which, by the way, includes the slipup that may have happened just a minute ago. But I'm telling you, do not let your mind stay on these things!

I want to remind you to move forward in forgiveness and grace. I gave My life so you could have this. I really want you to avail yourself of it! Remember that I'm constantly building and blessing My dear children—you!

Brand new places are being formed every moment, beautiful spots in barren spaces. I have great plans for you. So keep looking for the renewal. You will find it—it is in My creation all around, it is in you, it is in your children and in your closest relationships. Renewal is available through Me every day, every minute. Look for that.

Father God, thank You that You remember not my sin.
Renew my heart and mind today. Amen.

BEAUTY DAY BY DAY

*Therefore we do not lose heart. Though outwardly we are
wasting away, yet inwardly we are being renewed day by day.*

2 Corinthians 4:16 niv

Being a mom takes its physical toll on you every day, and I know there are many times when you look in the mirror and see that. It's no secret that you will decline physically as you age, but somehow it sneaks up on you, doesn't it?

I want you to know that while you can only limit the physical wear and tear, you are stronger and stronger internally as you grow in your knowledge of Me.

Keep focusing on the Good News of the Gospel, on grace, and on how I rose from the dead! Strengthen your heart with this, and share it with your children, family, friends, and neighbors—so that they too may come to know My saving grace.

Focus on the eternal beautiful life you will have with Me, rather than on the decay that occurs in this life, and you will encourage many others to share this hope with you, too, including your precious children!

*Lord, thank You that I do not need to worry about the physical
fading that is sure to happen in motherhood. Turn my eyes to
eternal things that I may be beautiful in Your sight. Amen.*

MOMMY TIME-OUT. . .IN THE BATHROOM

But the fruit of the [Holy] Spirit [the work which His presence
within accomplishes] is love, joy (gladness), peace, patience
(an even temper, forbearance), kindness, goodness (benevolence),
faithfulness, gentleness (meekness, humility), self-control
(self-restraint, continence). Against such things there is no law.
GALATIANS 5:22–23 AMP

This is quite a list of characteristics, isn't it? I want to encourage you right off, these are all things that yielding to the Holy Spirit will begin to produce in you. Not overnight, mind you, so give yourself time. It's a process.

When you come to the end of your patience with your children and self-control becomes an issue, come quickly to Me. You may need to shut the door behind you in the bathroom to get away for a minute and compose yourself, and that's okay! Then pray and listen.

Keep doing this (maybe not always the shutting-yourself-in-the-bathroom part), and little by little you will begin to notice yourself changing and growing. It will come!

Lord, I yield to You. Right now. I give You this moment
and this day. Give me a continual desire to be in the
process of being fruitful for You. Amen.

THE GROWING PROCESS

Guide older women into lives of reverence so they end up as neither gossips nor drunks, but models of goodness. By looking at them, the younger women will know how to love their husbands and children, be virtuous and pure, keep a good house, be good wives. We don't want anyone looking down on God's Message because of their behavior.
TITUS 2:3–5 MSG

D o you have an older woman in your life to model yourself after in your life of faith? If not, find one, and find a good one. Someone who loves Me and is striving to grow in Me, as well as someone who is honest about her struggles. You will find great benefit in your life as a mother by doing this. You can see how others have made it through tough times and learn from their mothering.

You will grow in your faith by being around someone more mature than you. It's so good to do this, and you'll end up thoroughly enjoying a mentor friendship like this.

Before you know it, you will see how you can help someone needing reinforcement on the journey, maybe a college-aged girl who needs encouragement or a brand-new mom. It's not about trying to be perfect for her; it's about encouraging one another along the way.

Lord, show me women ahead of me and behind me on the faith path, and give me the courage to learn from and encourage those in these roles. Amen.

EVERYDAY SACRIFICE

*Through Him then, let us continually offer up a sacrifice
of praise to God, that is, the fruit of lips that give thanks
to His name. And do not neglect doing good and
sharing, for with such sacrifices God is pleased.*

HEBREWS 13:15–16 NASB

You give up so much as a mother for the sake of your children. I want to applaud how you put yourself aside in so many ways. Not to the point of neglect, mind you, but to the extent that you point your children to Me and the sacrifice I made for them, and for you.

When your kids see your selflessness and all that you give in love, you are showing them a tangible example of Me. In this way you can lay out a measure of the Gospel story for them with your everyday life.

Experiencing sacrificial love given on their behalf is powerful. Receiving grace freely given in exchange for nothing—well, you're living it out with this one!

My love is going to shine through you, and your children will know who I am.

*Lord, give me the strength and faith I need today to sacrifice
with love for my children, that I would reflect You. Amen.*

MY STRENGTH

Therefore I am well content with weaknesses, with insults,
with distresses, with persecutions, with difficulties,
for Christ's sake; for when I am weak, then I am strong.
2 Corinthians 12:10 nasb

There are certainly weaknesses and distresses that make you feel weak as a mom, aren't there? I know it's hard to be okay with areas of life where you feel you come up short. Or with a trying situation you suddenly find yourself in, especially when your children may be impacted.

Here's the good news: whatever it is, I can be your strength. I can make up the difference between your shortfalls and your successes as a parent, no matter the cause. You may or may not have a long-term thorn in the flesh like my friend Paul did, but either way, if you depend on Me, you are going to be strong. I'm not saying not to work on getting better at things, but in times of weakness, I want you to always remember who I am.

You will begin to see these times as a gift because you will be drawn to Me in them and you will find sweet covering that only I can provide.

Lord, I see my shortcomings every day. I need You to be my strength
today. Enable me to be the mother You want me to be. Amen.

THANKFUL

Therefore, since we receive a kingdom which cannot be shaken, let us show gratitude, by which we may offer to God an acceptable service with reverence and awe.

HEBREWS 12:28 NASB

The more you can point out the things you are thankful for, the happier you are going to be. And I have to say, it is beautiful to see gratitude!

So name the things you are thankful for in front of your children and with your children. They will develop a sweet, appreciative attitude from this practice. There is so much to name—think about it. Your family, your home, your friends, your food, the many opportunities you have—the list is long!

Not the least of the items to give praise for is the immovable eternal kingdom you are a part of as one of My children. Share this with your kids. You will offer great hope for tomorrow and joy for today.

Lord, I am so grateful for Your love and eternal plan with great promise. Give me the clarity today to focus on what I am thankful for. Amen.

SPIRIT LIFT

Pray hard and long. Pray for your brothers and sisters.
Keep your eyes open. Keep each other's spirits up
so that no one falls behind or drops out.
Ephesians 6:18 msg

In your journey as a mother, there are many others alongside you who need your prayers and encouragement. You may easily notice your children's prayer needs but maybe not so easily your friends' or neighbors'.

It takes intentionality and alertness, really looking around in your everyday life to see the needs of others. But when you do this, you will be amazed at how much praying for or speaking kinds words to others will lift you up at the same time. You will feel good about helping in some way.

The other thing that will often surprise you is how much the people you forgot you helped will be there for you when you need it. Not that this is your motive to help them, but it just ends up blessing you back a hundredfold.

Every time you speak love into the lives of others, and to your children, you are making Me more real to them. It's beautiful!

Dear God, give me eyes to see the needs around me
and a willingness to reach out as I should,
that I would reflect You today. Amen.

IT ALL COUNTS

But thanks be to God, who gives us the victory through our
Lord Jesus Christ. Therefore, my beloved brethren, be steadfast,
immovable, always abounding in the work of the Lord,
knowing that your toil is not in vain in the Lord.
1 Corinthians 15:57–58 nasb

How many tasks do you complete every day as a mother that feel like striving after the wind? A lot, I know!

There are so many repetitive chores. It may seem like doing these one more time will not make a difference. You may get to thinking, *Why do I bother?*

But just hang on—I have encouraging news for you! I want you to know that not a single small thing that you do when you are looking to glorify Me in your work will be wasted. Not one.

I am the Master of using every little thing. All the menial jobs. The breakfasts, lunches, and dinners that blur together. The mountains of laundry and revolving door of dirt. The countless settling of arguments and calming of fears. All of these add up to something absolutely beautiful as you invest in the hearts and souls of your children. You pour into them love and sacrifice that are a reflection of Me.

Lord, today help me to push past the feelings of futility
that nag at me so that I can see the bigger picture
of mothering in a way that shines for You. Amen.

PRECIOUS LIFE

The Lord God who created the heavens and stretched them out, who created the earth and everything in it, who gives life and breath and spirit to everyone in all the world, he is the one who says to his Servant, the Messiah: "I the Lord have called you to demonstrate my righteousness."
ISAIAH 42:5–6 TLB

You know how you love to watch your children sleep? The rise and fall of their chests as they breathe peacefully is so precious. I know; I feel the same way about them and about you.

Your life is a masterpiece. It started with creating you and has continued with each breath. Now that you're a mother, so much beauty is unfolding as your children grow, and I am loving watching it all!

The way you love them and expand your faith is awesome. As you see them step out into places outside of home, it feels like your heart is out there walking around with legs.

That's how I feel about you.

Lord, thank You for each breath and for the great love You give my children and I. Help me not to take a moment for granted today. Amen.

STRONG MOTHERS

Finally, be strong in the Lord and in the strength of his might. Put on the whole armor of God, that you may be able to stand against the schemes of the devil.
EPHESIANS 6:10–11 ESV

When you feel weak, I can give you all the strength you need and more, and I'm so happy to do this for you!

Your children and the many demands of life may be wearing you out in a thousand ways today, but I want to help you. I love you and your children like crazy, and your work as a parent is so vital.

I have a motherhood arsenal of armor that is at your disposal. First of all, make it a daily practice to build yourself up in truth so that the lies of the Enemy won't stand a chance on you. Your faith will be a shield for you, protecting you from the Enemy's attacks. Your only offensive weapon is the sword of My Word, My message, given to you by the Holy Spirit (Ephesians 6:14–17). Keep using this armor, and teach your children to use it, too. In Me, you can be a strong family.

Lord God, I am weak in the face of all that is in front of me today. Give me strength by being my strength, that I would be the mother You would have me be today for my children. Amen.

ENCOURAGMENT FOR ALL

*Let us hold unswervingly to the hope we profess, for he who promised
is faithful. And let us consider how we may spur one another on toward
love and good deeds, not giving up meeting together, as some are in
the habit of doing, but encouraging one another.*
HEBREWS 10:23–25 NIV

The hope you have in Me is a very real thing; remembering this will get
you through a lot!

The challenges of motherhood, the decisions you have to make, and the
physical and emotional energy you exert daily can wear you right out. You
could start to feel alone and discouraged, but don't fall into that trap!

There are other moms all around you with similar struggles, and I want
to use you and your Christian sisters to encourage one another in your
faith. So when you feel a bit overwhelmed and want to turn inward with
sadness, resist.

Reach out instead. What you will find is that you will be just as blessed
by others as they are by you. Okay, maybe not by everyone! Be persistent
and patient in this. Find other moms at church, play groups, or Bible study.
Be a part of Christian community in your daily and weekly life. You and
your kids will be so glad you did!

*Lord, give me the strength and courage to reach out to
others, that I would be a blessing to them and to You. Amen.*

ENTRUSTED FULLY TO YOU

The LORD is my light and my salvation—whom shall I fear?
The LORD is the stronghold of my life—of whom shall I be afraid?
When the wicked advance against me to devour me, it is my
enemies and my foes who will stumble and fall.
PSALM 27:1–2 NIV

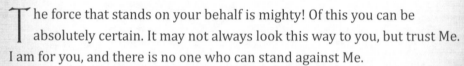

The force that stands on your behalf is mighty! Of this you can be absolutely certain. It may not always look this way to you, but trust Me. I am for you, and there is no one who can stand against Me.

So when you may be fearful for yourself or for your children, know that you can trust Me with all of it. The concerns you have for your children can be especially great. When they are out of your sight or battling an issue that is out of your control, it can be scary. But know this—every aspect of their well-being can be entrusted to My care. No matter what they do or where they go, I am able to protect them. Keep lifting them up to Me.

Lord God, today I give You my children. I entrust
their complete care to You, the only One who can
fully protect and bless them. Amen.

EVERYDAY OFFERING

So here's what I want you to do, God helping you: Take your
everyday, ordinary life—your sleeping, eating, going-to-work, and
walking-around life—and place it before God as an offering. Embracing
what God does for you is the best thing you can do for him.
ROMANS 12:1 MSG

My dear friend Paul says it well in this passage. It really is the simple acts in your normal life that I want to use, whatever normal is for you.

A regular day for you with the kids can mean running at breakneck speed after a sleepless night or enjoying a nice breakfast in your pj's with the kids saying adorable things that make you love life. It could be a day when the house is a real train wreck or a day when you are feeling really on top of things. It might be a packed day from 6:00 a.m. to 6:00 p.m., only to get home for your second shift of work at home, or a day you're home all day with the kids just relaxing and playing together.

You know how far the pendulum can swing; you don't know what a day will bring. But it's your regular day I can use for great things, one regular thing at a time. Whatever it is—I love when you give it to Me.

Lord, I give You the normal of this day, as crazy or as
calm as it may be. Make my ordinary extraordinary. Amen.

SEEING AND BEING IN HIM

Don't become so well-adjusted to your culture that you fit into it without even thinking. Instead, fix your attention on God. You'll be changed from the inside out. Readily recognize what he wants from you, and quickly respond to it. Unlike the culture around you, always dragging you down to its level of immaturity, God brings the best out of you, develops well-formed maturity in you.

ROMANS 12:2 MSG

You help your children to adjust well to a lot of things, or at least you try. This is all well and good unless you're not careful.

When it comes to your culture, be especially watchful. There are so many subtle things that seek to pull you and your children in. But if you just keep putting My Word up next to these things, you will know where it's great to fit in and where it really isn't. Teach your children the truth, and encourage them toward good decisions.

You'll get to praise them for good choices, but you will likely also help them adjust to not always being in the crowd they thought was cool. But you get it; it happens to you, too.

They will learn, just as you are learning, to love like I do and grow in faith and wisdom, becoming strong people who shine for Me.

Lord, give me clarity today to see and be in You. Amen.

LIVING IN GRACE

I'm speaking to you out of deep gratitude for all that God has given me, and especially as I have responsibilities in relation to you. Living then, as every one of you does, in pure grace, it's important that you not misinterpret yourselves as people who are bringing this goodness to God. No, God brings it all to you.

ROMANS 12:3 MSG

Y ou try to live your life well, in a way that is pleasing to Me. This can get misconstrued into a belief that somehow My love and grace can be earned. But that would be the opposite of grace.

So don't get confused! Because of what I have done for you by dying on the cross and rising from the dead, there is no act that needs to be done to get to Me. No supermom behavior or church volunteering or following all the rules. None of that.

Rather, it's simple faith, a posture of the heart.

Because the work that earned your grace is done—you get to live in Me, and as a result you will want to do what is good and true.

Lord God, let me abide in You this day, that I may live in grace and offer grace, genuinely desiring to do what is good and true. Amen.

EYES AND TOES

So since we find ourselves fashioned into all these excellently formed
and marvelously functioning parts in Christ's body, let's just go ahead and
be what we were made to be, without enviously or pridefully comparing
ourselves with each other, or trying to be something we aren't.
ROMANS 12:6 MSG

You are a part of a huge body of people, My Church. It's tough to really get your mind to see this. I mean, My Church is huge. You can start to feel small in the mix of so many people and wonder if your job matters. Sometimes you look at people you admire for their work and you feel bad that you aren't like them.

I have to tell you, I made you to be you. To be anyone else would be like a toe trying to be an eye. Now that sounds funny, doesn't it? But you get the idea—it's impossible.

I have a purpose for you and each of your children, too. You are each tailor made.

So resist envy and pride, and just keep growing and helping your kids grow. . .and let a toe be a toe!

Father God, thank You for the place You have for me.
Show me today how to encourage my children to be exactly
the spectacular people You created them to be. Amen.

YIELDING TO OTHERS

Love from the center of who you are; don't fake it. Run
for dear life from evil; hold on for dear life to good. Be good
friends who love deeply; practice playing second fiddle.
ROMANS 12:9–10 MSG

Giving preference to others isn't natural. It's something you will learn and grow in.

Being a mother sure forces you to put yourself aside though, doesn't it? So don't begrudge what you give up for your kids. It will teach you a lot—not that you should get trampled over by yielding, but you simply put others ahead of yourself in love. Serve them the way I serve you. The great thing is that when you love your kids and others the way I love you, it will transform things. You will find a depth of relationship with Me and with others that you didn't have before.

Oh, and don't worry, if it isn't already clear—I will take care of you, too. You can be sure of that!

Lord, it is so hard many days to put myself aside for others.
Today help me do just that, one moment at a time. Give me
the deep and genuine love that only You can give. Amen.

CARING FOR YOU

Don't burn out; keep yourselves fueled and aflame.
Be alert servants of the Master, cheerfully expectant.
Don't quit in hard times; pray all the harder.
Help needy Christians; be inventive in hospitality.
ROMANS 12:11–13 MSG

I want to encourage you to do the things you need to recharge so you can be effective in your work as a mother and everything else you do.

You already know that I am your strength. But you need to realize that if you don't do the things in your power to take care of yourself, you will limit what I can do through your life.

So get the rest you should when you can. That may mean letting a mess or two sit until the next day. Feed your body well, and take care of every aspect of your physical being the best you know how. Continue to learn about all that I created—your body, food, and plants that can help you. There is a wealth of power and healing in what I have made. Just keep working at it and you will have the health and strength you need.

Lord, give me the discipline I need to care for myself
so that I can be the best caregiver possible
to my children and others. Amen.

TEACHING THEM ABOUT FALLENNESS

Don't hit back; discover beauty in everyone. If you've got it in you, get along with everybody. Don't insist on getting even; that's not for you to do. "I'll do the judging," says God. "I'll take care of it."
ROMANS 12:17–19 MSG

These are the things you teach your children and that you've likely heard since childhood yourself.

Be nice. Don't punch back. Find the good in others. Try to get along with everyone. And of course the best one, "Revenge belongs to God."

It can be humbling when you have taught your children these things and then they take notice of you being upset or bickering with someone. They may overhear a judgmental remark you made, and they may then wonder if you really mean what you said.

How do you recover from these low moments?

With humility, that's how. Be honest when you have erred in front of your children. Own your stuff, and ask for forgiveness. Talk about it with them.

Now you've really taught them something!

Lord, help me to be forthcoming with my children about my faults when it is called for. Give me the self-awareness and courage I need to teach them well in this fallen state. Amen.

HE KNOWS MY HEART

All the ways of a man are clean in his own sight,
but the LORD weighs the motives.
PROVERBS 16:2 NASB

Have you ever had your child do something very sweet for you only to find that he or she wanted something from you? When your child's motive is far from the appearance of things, it can be disheartening, can't it?

Doubly disheartening are the times when you do this yourself! Don't you feel awful about it? I know. I know your heart.

What you did seemed completely fine at the time. You looked at only the good in it. Your eyes saw just this.

Somehow the master trickster was you. Don't get Me wrong, the Enemy loves to play with you, so ultimately he's involved. But you will manage to trick yourself into thinking that some behaviors you choose are perfectly good, when in actuality your motive is far from good.

It can be ugly.

Nothing will remind you to keep this in check like parenting, and that's good news. Every time you challenge your kids in loving ways to examine their motives, you are checking in with yourself.

This is some great accountability for you!

Dear God, help me to quickly see when my motive is off
base so I will be a good example for my children. Amen.

EMERGING

*Search me, O God, and know my heart; try me and know
my anxious thoughts; and see if there be any hurtful
way in me, and lead me in the everlasting way.*
Psalm 139:23–24 nasb

What are the nagging thoughts that sometimes trouble you? What sits heavy in your heart? I want to help you with those.

The transformation of faith is a process. Little by little you will realize things that you need to work on or work through. I can show them to you as soon as you are ready, and I am super happy to help you!

Just ask and I'll get to work with you. I can show you things that you haven't seen before or habits you didn't realize you had. Sometimes I'll show you something hurtful that you did and that never crossed your mind before. When you see things for yourself, you will want forgiveness, and you'll want to change. I can help you with all of that.

Engaging in this process will be a bit like the butterfly emerging from his cocoon. The transformation is beautiful.

*Lord, take a searchlight to my heart, and show
me the things I need to see, that I would be the
person my children need today. Amen.*

KNOWING THE ONE WHO NEVER WEARIES

The LORD is the everlasting God, the Creator of the ends of the earth.
He will not grow tired or weary, and his understanding no one can fathom.
He gives strength to the weary and increases the power of the weak.
ISAIAH 40:28–29 NIV

The state of being slightly tattered and tired as a mom can quickly snowball into complete exhaustion. You've been there. Sometimes it's satisfying exhaustion; other times it's disheartening. Either way, I can give you the energy and creativity you need wherever you find yourself.

It may help if you have a bigger picture of who I am.

I created every star and hung them all in the great expanse with care. Every planet and galaxy was crafted by Me. I made your galaxy, the Milky Way. On only one of those planets, I provided a sun and moon with exactly the heat and light needed to sustain My crowning creation, mankind. Made in My image, humans are unique. They have been given the freedom to choose Me. I sustain them with all they need and love them beyond their wildest imaginations.

Lord God, bolster my strength today in Your mighty power.
Thank You that You are more than able to
give me all I need today. Amen.

FREEDOM TO CHOOSE HIM

*"I'm sending you off to open the eyes of the outsiders so they can
see the difference between dark and light, and choose light, see
the difference between Satan and God, and choose God."*
ACTS 26:17 MSG

Have you ever been in love with someone who didn't love you back? Rejection is one of the most painful prices of love. The happiest and healthiest relationships exist when someone loves you back.

That's why I give you the freedom to reject Me. It can be painful, that's for sure. But it is so worth it. The beauty of reciprocal love is indescribable and so precious to Me.

You have begun to teach your children this freedom every day when you love them regardless of their behavior. When you discipline their bad decisions, they are in the place to choose whether they love you for the moment. How many times have you heard, "I don't like you! You're mean!"

You know who the mature person is in those moments, don't you? You get to teach them so many things. The difference between like and love, for starters, and that true love is offered in freedom, not coercion.

*Lord, let me shine beautifully in You today, that my children
and others I encounter will want to choose You. Amen.*

LETTING GO

*Even youths grow tired and weary, and young men stumble
and fall; but those who hope in the LORD will renew their
strength. They will soar on wings like eagles; they will run
and not grow weary, they will walk and not be faint.*
ISAIAH 40:30–31 NIV

Every day you are inching your little ones closer to the edge of the nest and helping them learn to fly. It's a long process, but little by little you are keeping this in mind.

One day you will release them to fly under My care. Don't worry, they'll likely circle back to you many times as they figure things out. You will miss them when they've flown out, but you'll know you did your job well when they begin to really put their trust in Me on their own.

I know it's hard to imagine this happening when your children are little, but it comes before you realize where the years have gone.

So keep the goal in sight, one bit of responsibility at a time. One faith lesson at a time. One life lesson at a time. One prayer at a time. I'll be with you until they stretch their wings out wide, and I'll be there to help them soar.

*Dear God, give me the wisdom I need for the letting-go
process. Today I release my children entirely to You.
I need You entirely, and so do they. Amen.*

GIVE IT ALL

Don't fret or worry. Instead of worrying, pray. Let petitions and praises shape your worries into prayers, letting God know your concerns. Before you know it, a sense of God's wholeness, everything coming together for good, will come and settle you down. It's wonderful what happens when Christ displaces worry at the center of your life.

PHILIPPIANS 4:6–7 MSG

How quickly an observation becomes a worry, am I right? It can come in like a storm over a mountain, blindsiding you in no time.

One small thing you notice—it could be something as small as a bug bite on your child. And before you know it, you're looking up the brown recluse spider bite online. Don't get Me wrong, knowledge is good, but I want to give you a solid foundation under everything you do. Remember that I love you like crazy—I love when you come to Me for help!

Start with prayer. Just talk to Me. Ask Me for help. I will give you what you need. It may be guidance, knowledge, or wisdom to know just what to do. But the overarching thing I'll give you is peace. I can give you a sense of calm in any storm that sneaks up on you.

*Lord, I give You the worries that lurk in me today.
Give me the calm confidence I need—
the kind only You can provide. Amen.*

MOTHER'S LIFE-GIVING WORDS

*Good friend, follow your father's good advice; don't wander off
from your mother's teachings. Wrap yourself in them from head
to foot; wear them like a scarf around your neck. Wherever you
walk, they'll guide you; whenever you rest, they'll guard you; when
you wake up, they'll tell you what's next. For sound advice is a
beacon, good teaching is a light, moral discipline is a life path.*
PROVERBS 6:20–23 MSG

No pressure, but the path of your child's life is substantially influenced by your words and instruction. Yeah, no pressure!

Aren't you glad you've got a good teacher yourself? I will give you everything you need for your beloved children; I really will. Every little lesson. Every good word. Every tiny bit of truth and encouragement that will steer them right. You'll find it in My Word and in My still, small voice. You'll hear it when you take the time to listen, even if that's when your head hits the pillow.

Just keep pouring the truth into them with all the love you can muster and you will have done well.

*Lord, today show me the truth. I need You and Your Word
for my children. Guide me for their sakes. Amen.*

WISDOM IN GOOD COUNSEL

The empty-headed treat life as a plaything; the perceptive grasp
its meaning and make a go of it. Refuse good advice and watch
your plans fail; take good counsel and watch them succeed.
PROVERBS 15:21–22 MSG

Your head sure isn't empty! You are grabbing onto everything you can get as you learn to be a better mother all the time. One of the many great gifts I've given you in your journey is your family in faith.

I will use your brothers and sisters many times to help you in wonderful ways. Sometimes it will be a word I want them to share with you. Other times you need to hear what I've done in another mother's life so you are encouraged in your own walk.

So don't be afraid of this. Be attentive and listen. There will be some beautiful wisdom and encouragement that comes from My people. Humble yourself, and prepare to be blessed. You will find favor as you seek My wisdom in the stories of the big, amazing family you are a part of.

Lord God, give me eyes to see from whom You want me to receive wise counsel.
Thank You for working through others on my behalf. Amen.

DEATH, WHERE IS YOUR VICTORY?

"If you practice what I'm telling you, you'll
never have to look death in the face."
JOHN 8:51 MSG

I f you haven't yet had to endure the loss of someone you love dearly, unless it happens to you first, it *is* something you will sadly experience. Now that sounds morbid, doesn't it? But I tell you, if you and your loved ones know Me, you need not fear death.

My children come straight to me in eternity when their earthly time is done, and what a beautiful reunion it is. How I love these precious times of exceeding joy!

Of course it is heart wrenching in this earthly life to lose someone you love, and I hurt seeing your sadness. I clearly remember that pain. But if you put your trust in Me, you can be confident of your destiny. You'll gain a beautiful eternal perspective that you didn't have before.

You need to remember that I put death in the grave with Me and then rose from the dead—for good! I did it to conquer death and sin once and for all. You are the beneficiary of it all!

◇◇◇◇◇◇◇◇◇◇◇◇◇◇◇◇◇◇◇◇◇◇◇◇◇◇◇◇◇◇◇◇◇◇◇◇◇◇

Lord, help me to trust in You fully in times of loss.
No matter how great the pain, give me clear sight
of eternal hope that is far greater. Amen.

SPRING OF HOPE

Behold, the winter is past; the rain is over and gone.
The flowers appear on the earth, the time of singing has
come, and the voice of the turtledove is heard in our land.

SONG OF SOLOMON 2:11–12 ESV

No matter how much many parts of your life can feel like a deep-freeze winter, the hope of spring is always there.

When circumstances with your children storm at you in a snowy whiteout way, when the pileup of problems drifts over you, remember this hope: I will always work something beautiful out of whatever is happening. Whether it's a deep heart issue or a seemingly small detail of the day, I'm working it out for you. You may not get to see the result as clearly or as timely as the bright yellow tulips of spring, but rest assured, spring is coming in your winter nonetheless.

One way or another I will bring song and rejoicing to you and to your children.

Lord, thank You for the promise of new life
in the areas of my life that seem dark and dead
right now. I trust You with these times. Amen.

MY BIG OL' BOTTLE OF TEARS

You have taken account of my wanderings; put my tears in
Your bottle. Are they not in Your book? Then my enemies will turn
back in the day when I call; this I know, that God is for me.
PSALM 56:8–9 NASB

No eye-welling that pools to tears goes unnoticed by Me. Not a single one. Each droplet that slides quietly down your cheek registers with Me. I know when you hurt. I see when you are troubled. You hurt most deeply for your children when there is a problem.

What I want you to realize is that I hurt when you hurt. The same way your heart aches when your children are experiencing trouble, this is how I feel about you.

Everywhere your heart breaks or chips, each time you think it will split wide open, it's not escaping me. I'm capturing it all, and one day you will see every painstaking detail of care that has surrounded you each moment of your life. Because I love you.

Father God, give me the confidence to walk boldly in my
faith today, knowing that every moment is under Your care. Amen.

DYING TO SELF AND GIVING LIFE

"This is My commandment, that you love one another,
just as I have loved you. Greater love has no one than
this, that one lay down his life for his friends."
JOHN 15:12–13 NASB

You know how your kids mean more than anything to you? You'd throw yourself in front of a train if that's what you had to do to save them. I know. I get it. That's how I feel about you (and them).

Yet, as much as you would easily sacrifice your life for your kids to rescue them, you are doing that on a daily basis by giving your energy, love, and time to them. Every increment of a moment is precious sacrifice. This is harder than a single act of rescue. This requires you to live in real-time all the time.

Want to take it a level deeper? Lay down your life for your friends, too, and now you're thoroughly letting My love shine.

I absolutely love watching love in action!

Lord, thank You for the example of sacrifice You are
to me. Help me to follow Your earthly example of
living for others daily and dying to self. Amen.

SET FREE

*Let all bitterness and wrath and anger and clamor and
slander be put away from you, along with all malice.
Be kind to one another, tenderhearted, forgiving
one another, as God in Christ forgave you.*
EPHESIANS 4:31–32 ESV

People will do some awful things toward you and your children. Things that certainly seem to warrant telling lots of people about it or, at minimum, having an attitude toward them.

After all, they're trying to hurt your children. They should pay, right?

Well, you can see I set you up to answer that one with a big, dreary "Wrong."

I know—it's hard. But here's the thing—you have been forgiven by Me. For everything. Likewise, as a partaker in My grace, you get to practice extending that forgiveness to others. No worries, I don't expect you to nail it every time.

Just keep asking Me to show you the way and give you what you need. I will. You can do this.

The beautiful thing is that when you offer forgiveness, it seems like you're setting the offender free. The reality is, you're setting both of you free.

*Lord, help me to forgive those who have hurt me and my
children, that I might be an example of Your great grace. Amen.*

EXPIRE NO MORE

*Blessed be the God and Father of our Lord Jesus Christ,
who according to His great mercy has caused us to be born again
to a living hope through the resurrection of Jesus Christ from the
dead, to obtain an inheritance which is imperishable and undefiled
and will not fade away, reserved in heaven for you.*

1 PETER 1:3–4 NASB

You have so many things that expire in short order. The fresh fruit you just bought—its days are numbered. The sunset I will give you tonight—it will go away quickly. The next laugh you will share with your children—over in moments.

You can be glad that I give you much richer things that never fade. Salvation, for starters. You have a hope that is always there, no matter what.

Eternity, where your forever inheritance is, is not going away.

Everlasting hope—that's what I give you today and every day. This way the disappearing things you do every day for your children will not discourage you—not for long anyway.

*Lord, remind me of the unending Hope I have in You today,
that I can happily endure the expirations of today. Amen.*

PEACE AND PROTECTION AMID EVIL

*Many are saying, "Who will show us any good?" Lift up the light of
Your countenance upon us, O LORD! You have put gladness in my heart,
more than when their grain and new wine abound. In peace I will both
lie down and sleep, for You alone, O LORD, make me to dwell in safety.*
PSALM 4:6–8 NASB

The world you live in is a real mess, isn't it? Some say they don't want to bring children into such a place. Hatred does not run low, and deceit is rampant. You see it all over the place. Misguided parents bring up children who lack boundaries and truth. Abuse and abduction of precious young people cause many to be fearful of doing what you are doing—parenting.

But I tell you, in Me peace reigns no matter where you find yourself! My protection prevails over you. Rest and restoration are yours, in Me. I am watching over you and your children every minute of every day.

*Lord God, today I trust You with all that comes my way,
knowing that You know what You're doing.
You work on my behalf. Amen.*

CONTROLLED COURAGE

For the Spirit God gave us does not make us timid,
but gives us power, love and self-discipline.
2 TIMOTHY 1:7 NIV

There are times when you don't want to push your way, and you wonder if you should. So you yield to others and later find that you were the one who should have pressed; you had the wisdom.

The Spirit who has been given to you is immensely strong and controlled. He will never steer you wrong. So just listen to His bold direction and go courageously forward, careful to follow rather than running ahead.

Share what you know you should. With your children. With your neighbors. With the arguing strangers in the store. With the disgruntled coworker. With family members who may not want to hear it. With church family who need firm words of love. And sometimes that boldness will mean saying nothing at all, but you'll know.

Just share the gifts and words that have been given to you. The Holy Spirit will guide you, and I am with you.

Father God, give me ears to hear Your Spirit, a heart willing to obey,
and the courage to do all You give me to do today. Amen.

CHOICES THAT GIVE LIFE TODAY

I place before you Life and Death, Blessing and Curse.
Choose life so that you and your children will live.
And love GOD, your God, listening obediently to him,
firmly embracing him. Oh yes, he is life itself.
DEUTERONOMY 30:19–20 MSG

Every day is full of choices for you as a mom. Largely, it's you who gets to pick how things will go. What will you choose?

You can opt to face issues or numb yourself. Encourage or discourage. Forgive or hold a grudge. Be joyful or bitter. Listen or ignore. Dance or slump over. Build up or tear down. See the beauty or the ugliness. Be a light or dim it. Fuel dreams or dampen them. Smile in their eager faces or frown. Add energy or drain it. Give or take away. Pray or complain. Fix it or let it break down. Heal or let it fester. Travel light or carry tons of baggage.

With Me by your side, infusing life into you, you can choose the way of life. Go do that today!

Lord, You see how I fall short, but today You give me
a clean slate. Help me to choose Your ways today,
that I might bless and build up my children. Amen.

ON COURSE IN THE WORD

You're blessed when you stay on course, walking steadily on the road revealed by GOD. You're blessed when you follow his directions, doing your best to find him. That's right—you don't go off on your own; you walk straight along the road he set. You, GOD, prescribed the right way to live; now you expect us to live it.
PSALM 119:1–4 MSG

Sometimes you wonder if you're on the right path, don't you? You second-guess the decisions you've made on behalf of your family. Every decision matters. Every choice has gravity, and you want to make the right ones.

How can you know?

The truth I've given in My Word should not be underrated. It's chock-full of great knowledge and history; all that I placed there is for you to use in your circumstances today. That's right, today! Not only in the distant future, but right now.

So get in there and invite Me to study with you. I'll show you so much practical wisdom for you and your family. You'll be amazed!

Father God, show me today in Your Word what I need to parent well. Then add wisdom to knowledge, that I may appropriately apply Your Word to my life. Amen.

POETS, BUILDERS, AND ACCOUNTANTS

"As for Asher, his food shall be rich, and he will yield royal dainties. Naphtali is a doe let loose, he gives beautiful words. Joseph is a fruitful bough, a fruitful bough by a spring; its branches run over a wall."
GENESIS 49:20–22 NASB

What are your children? One might be a chef, another a writer, another a soldier or an engineer. I know the gifts bestowed to them and love to watch them grow in all of these. Each precious child is unique, complex, and beautiful.

You get the fun job of helping them see their strengths so they can develop them. The same way that I help you with this, and put others in your life to help you see your gifts, you help your kids find what they love. Then you can create opportunities for them to explore and develop with their strengths and desires. It's like watching a butterfly slowly come out of its cocoon. You're going to love it almost as much as I do!

Lord, give me eyes to see my children's gifts, that I might be a catalyst for growth in their blossoming lives. Amen.

ROAD MAP THROUGH DARKNESS

*How can a young person live a clean life? By carefully reading
the map of your Word. I'm single-minded in pursuit of you; don't
let me miss the road signs you've posted. I've banked your promises
in the vault of my heart so I won't sin myself bankrupt.*
PSALM 119:9–11 MSG

In today's culture so many think it's impossible for young people to live lives pleasing to Me. But I'm telling you that there is nothing in your culture that is new to Me. Nothing shocks Me!

Your children can walk in a clear, beautiful path, even amid the cloudiness that may surround them.

Encourage them in My Word every chance you get. Share with them the truth, and help them see how it stands up against every lie the Enemy seeks to plant in their hearts and minds. Don't shelter them from everything, but give them what they can handle so they learn how to live well. Keep pointing them to Me, that My Light might reflect in their lives. This way the darkness is illumined, and they can walk wisely in it.

*Dear God, give me truth for my children today. Let me reflect
Your love and grace, that they would choose Your way. Amen.*

CREATOR HEALER

For You formed my inward parts; You wove me in my mother's womb.
I will give thanks to You, for I am fearfully and wonderfully made;
wonderful are Your works, and my soul knows it very well.
PSALM 139:13–14 NASB

What physical needs do you have today? Is there a mysterious health condition or a severe sickness causing hopelessness for you? Perhaps you are simply weary, physically spent from the demands of life.

I know exactly what it is that ails you. I made you and can see the detail inside you better than any MRI or CAT scan out there. You were beautifully formed, all with intention and purpose, and so were your children.

Ask Me for what you need. I want to provide for you and give you all that benefits you and your dear family. But try to remember that I will use each circumstance in mysterious ways that may seem quite foreign to you. Sometimes there will be a miracle healing, other times a lingering situation. It's hard, I know.

Trust Me.

Lord, give me the faith to trust all that You bring to my life today,
especially when I don't understand Your reasons. Amen.

EXPECTANT

He knows us far better than we know ourselves, knows
our pregnant condition, and keeps us present before God.
That's why we can be so sure that every detail in our lives
of love for God is worked into something good.
ROMANS 8:27–28 MSG

How about your longings and desires? The things that hang, linger, and hold with expectation in every fiber of you.

You know them. Does it help you to know that I know each of these through and through, better than you do? You don't have to feel alone in your most desperate of desires. You never need to be without hope. I am continually bringing these before My Father on your behalf. Every aching for what is best in your most important relationships, every concern for your children's future, for emotional and spiritual health—everything. I'm on it.

My Father always does what is absolutely best for you and your kids. Even though it may not make sense at the time and can hurt, you've got to trust Me on this one. I know. I asked Him to remove the suffering of the cross if it were possible, but it wasn't. And look at the beauty it all brought—you have eternal hope because of it. The cross made a way for you and your kids to be with Me, now and forever.

Father, help me to keep giving You my great
expectations and deepest longings, trusting that
You will work them all toward the best end. Amen.

GRACE TO FAIL

If we confess our sins, He is faithful and righteous to forgive us our sins and to cleanse us from all unrighteousness. If we say that we have not sinned, we make Him a liar and His word is not in us.
1 John 1:9–10 nasb

You know when you're feeling bad about something you did? You know it was wrong, and you feel awful about it.

The same way you tell your children not to be afraid to come to you with anything, I tell you, come to Me with everything! Every action that you know fell short, every bit of gossip you passed on as a prayer request, every tiny manipulative thing you pulled off with wrong motive. You feel it in your spirit right away. The faster you come to Me with it, the faster you'll move on in forgiveness and freedom.

This is the grace I give you to live in daily. Live fully and step out, not intentionally in sin, of course, but know that you're bound to fall down. It's okay. It's the same thing you encourage in your kids; you give them the grace to try, which always must include the grace to fail.

Lord, help me be an example of humility and grace for my children today. Amen.

SAFE AND STRONG

God is our refuge and strength, a very present help in trouble. Therefore we will not fear, though the earth should change and though the mountains slip into the heart of the sea; though its waters roar and foam, though the mountains quake at its swelling pride. Selah. There is a river whose streams make glad the city of God.

PSALM 46:1–4 NASB

One thing you can be sure will never change is that things are constantly changing.

You see it all the time. Weather patterns fluctuate and baffle the experts. Tsunamis and hurricanes devastate. Monstrous tornadoes wipe out entire towns. So many live in fear, but I don't want you to be one of them!

I give you a river of life always accessible and refreshing to your very soul. Camp out along its banks, and drink of the clear, clean water. Sleep in peace here on soft grasses under the light of the moon. Awaken rested and strong for the work I have given you. Your life is beautiful.

Lord, be my strength today, and refresh me in mothering right when I need it. Amen.

HIS EXTRAVAGANT WORK IN YOUR LIFE

*I ask—ask the God of our Master, Jesus Christ, the God of glory—
to make you intelligent and discerning in knowing him personally,
your eyes focused and clear, so that you can see exactly what it is he is
calling you to do, grasp the immensity of this glorious way of life he
has for his followers, oh, the utter extravagance of his work in us
who trust him—endless energy, boundless strength!*
 Ephesians 1:18 msg

The beautiful energy of your children seems to know no bounds, right? And the times when their sweet giggles combine with your love—that makes an incredible day!

This is a picture of how wonderfully I will work through your life experiences every time you trust Me. There are countless ways I want to work that will be like finding treasure. It could be a simple exchange with other moms at school, and I may be able to reach someone through you or one of your kids. It could be a crisis one of your neighbors is having, and because you bring Me with you there is a conversation you just can't believe!

So keep going in trust, in Me—I want to keep surprising you with what I'll do!

*Lord, show me today where You want to use me,
as a mother, as a friend, as a neighbor. Amen.*

MOTHERING BEYOND HOME

Pure and undefiled religion in the sight of our God
and Father is this: to visit orphans and widows in their
distress, and to keep oneself unstained by the world.
JAMES 1:27 NASB

Your children are blessed to have a mother who cares for them as you do. You see the young ones who are hurting for lack of a mother, a mother who is oftentimes not exactly gone, just not there for them.

It could be your young neighbor who needs you, your child's friend, or a little relative. In any case, you have opportunity to encourage these children, to just show My love through your life.

You have no idea how much including them in your family activities from time to time will make a beautiful impact on them. Who knows what it will be that they see, forgiveness in action, grace, simple kindness, sacrificial love, or joy they've never known. There are countless ways you can speak My love into the lives of others.

Lord, bless me in my efforts to reach out to other children
while I mother my own, that You would be fully known
by the many people You bring into my life. Amen.

WHAT'S NEXT?

"And the LORD will continually guide you, and satisfy your desire in scorched places, and give strength to your bones; and you will be like a watered garden, and like a spring of water whose waters do not fail."
ISAIAH 58:11 NASB

Wondering about a big decision or which direction you should turn? People ask Me all the time about what to do next, and I love it!

There are so many things that demand decision. Which school? More school? Which job? No job? Where to live, and which relationships to invest in? You may wonder if a longing you have is in line with what I would have you do. There is no shortage of such questions.

Whatever it is, just ask Me and I will guide you, of that you can be sure (Jeremiah 33:3). I understand that sometimes you won't think to ask until you are in a desert sort of place. That works better at times—you'll appreciate the refreshing word I'll give you even more! Sometimes I'll speak to you through another, sometimes directly to your heart. Sometimes words will jump off a page as if they were written just for you. I'm pretty creative, though, so don't look for just one way that I'll give you the guidance you need. Just look to Me and wait for it.

Lord, give me ears to hear You, and guide me today. Amen.

PUTTING PROMOTION IN HIS HANDS

So be content with who you are, and don't put on airs. God's strong hand is on you; he'll promote you at the right time. Live carefree before God; he is most careful with you.

1 PETER 5:6–7 MSG

There are times when others push ahead on their own, forcing promotion of themselves. They seem to get much further ahead as a result. But I'm telling you, don't do it this way.

Instead, be glad for your progress exactly where you are, and remember that I'm continually building you up. You have freedom in Me to blossom and branch out. You're getting exactly the water, wind, sunshine, and pruning you need to flourish.

Whether it's in your work as a mother, your job, your volunteer work, or your aspirations—opportunities will come at just the right time. Keep leaning into Me, and they will come.

Father God, give me contentment with where You have me today, and give me the faith and courage to take the next step without worrying about what I perceive my reward should be. Amen.

HOLD IT

If anyone thinks himself to be religious, and yet does not bridle his tongue but deceives his own heart, this man's religion is worthless.
JAMES 1:26 NASB

You know how bad you feel when you've let your words run out of you like your baby's spit-up. Yeah, it's pretty icky!

It didn't seem so bad right before you said it; seemed like it would feel good to get it out, actually. Afterward, though, you started thinking about how awful you'd feel if that person heard you, and then—would it get back to them? Oh my, then you realized all the people you needed to apologize to for this offense. Why hadn't you just kept your mouth shut, you wonder.

Self-control is no easy thing, is it? Try this—apply My golden rule. Think about how bad you feel when something negative is said about you. But above all else, know how much it grieves My heart to see My children talking against one another. It's the same way you feel when your children are being mean to one another.

I'm not saying you can't speak the truth when needed—of course not. You should speak directly with someone if there is something that needs to be addressed (Matthew 18:15–17), but treat one another with love and respect.

Lord, give me the restraint I need to hold my tongue and honor others, showing the kind of love and mercy that You show me. Amen.

THE ONGOING CONVERSATION

*Rejoice always; pray without ceasing; in everything give
thanks; for this is God's will for you in Christ Jesus.*
1 Thessalonians 5:16–18 nasb

Do you get worn out with the constant bombardment of requests
from your children? They really need a lot from you, don't they?

I understand, but you can rest easy knowing that I don't ever get weary
from your requests. Remember, I'm the unlimited God who never needs
to sleep. In fact, I want you to come to Me as often as you can. Keep the
conversation going and the requests coming. It can be a 24–7 thing, truly!

It doesn't have to be just quiet time alone with Me, though that is
great, too. But talking and listening to Me anytime is a wonderful way to
move through the day. Give Me your concerns and plans as soon as you
awake in the morning. Chat with Me while you're having breakfast. Include
Me in the conversation with your kids. I just love that! And, of course,
remember that conversation includes plenty of time for listening.

*Lord God, I am walking and talking through this day with You.
Show me how to better include You in everything I do. Amen.*

STANDING IN THE GAP

*In the same way the Spirit also helps our weakness; for we do not
know how to pray as we should, but the Spirit Himself intercedes
for us with groanings too deep for words; and He who searches
the hearts knows what the mind of the Spirit is, because He
intercedes for the saints according to the will of God.*

ROMANS 8:26–27 NASB

For those who have known the grief of losing a child, you know extreme
agony. This is similar in ways to how My Father felt when I died on the
cross. He knows this grief intimately.

In times of devastating loss of any kind, you will often lose sight of
how to even begin to pray. You may be at a loss for words or even rational
thought. You may only be capable of yelling at Me. That's really okay—
I'm quite big enough to handle anything. The Spirit knows just how to
intercede for you, too, so don't worry if you don't have the words in your
times of great trouble.

Whether you've been there, are there, or will be there, We've got you
covered—even in the times when you don't perceive great trouble.

*Lord, the things that baffle me, overwhelm me, and cause me to lose
my bearings—thank You for seeing me through them, and for
Your Holy Spirit who prays on my behalf this day and always. Amen.*

SNEAK ATTACK

Be of sober spirit, be on the alert. Your adversary, the devil, prowls around like a roaring lion, seeking someone to devour. But resist him, firm in your faith, knowing that the same experiences of suffering are being accomplished by your brethren who are in the world.
1 Peter 5:8–9 nasb

Has something just snuck up on you and you didn't even see it coming, like a bad habit or a situation with someone you thought had pure motives? The Enemy is good at the sneak attack!

You can make it, though. There's no need to get overwhelmed. Practice being watchful and steadfast each day in your relationships, with your children, in your work, and in everything else. I'm certainly not saying I want you to be paranoid—no! Just be as aware as you can, and cover your decisions in prayer. You are part of a strong family, too, so know that you're never alone.

One more thing: nothing takes Me by surprise, so stay close to Me. You'll be fine!

Father, give me the faith I need for today, knowing that You are much bigger than the schemes the Enemy plots against me. Amen.

FIRM, STEADFAST, LOVING, AND KIND—ALWAYS

O give thanks to the LORD, for He is good;
for His lovingkindness is everlasting.
1 CHRONICLES 16:34 NASB

The affirmation, goodness, and kindness that the people in your life give you are fickle. Even when they're people who love you dearly and are faithfully committed to you, they will fail you. They're human, after all.

My loving-kindness, on the other hand, cannot be exhausted. It doesn't hinge on how I feel about a host of other things that are swirling around Me. It will not depend on if I liked the lunch you packed Me or not. It matters not how the day has gone up until this point, or if I thought you did something just right or not.

I will be constant in My love and devotion for you, for your children, for your family, and for every inconsistent person in your life. Holding fast, today and forever.

Lord, help me to depend on Your love and kindness today,
over that of others, that I would be more consistent
in the way I love others. Amen.

INFLUENCE AND LEADERSHIP

"So you'll go out in joy, you'll be led into a whole and complete life.
The mountains and hills will lead the parade, bursting with song. All
the trees of the forest will join the procession, exuberant with applause.
No more thistles, but giant sequoias, no more thornbushes, but stately
pines—monuments to me, to GOD, living and lasting evidence of GOD."
ISAIAH 55:12–13 MSG

Do you ever wonder if you are providing enough faith influence and leadership to lead your children to Me?

I want to reassure you that if you rely on My Word and make your decisions based on truth and love, you are on the right path. You just keep putting Me first, and seek the counsel of wise Christ-followers when you need it. Choose humble teachers who submit to Me to teach your family how to keep growing in your faith, and of course be a humble teacher yourself, always learning.

Over time, one day like this at a time, you will become a source of strength for others seeking as you did when you were young in your faith. What a joy it is when this happens!

Father God, move me forward with strength today as I provide godly
influence for my children—that they would choose You, too. Amen.

THE WORD WILL MAKE YOU FLOURISH

"Just as rain and snow descend from the skies and don't go back until they've watered the earth, doing their work of making things grow and blossom, producing seed for farmers and food for the hungry, so will the words that come out of my mouth not come back empty-handed. They'll do the work I sent them to do, they'll complete the assignment I gave them."
Isaiah 55:10–11 MSG

What do you need from the Word today? Maybe it's something on discipline for your children—that's certainly an ongoing issue throughout their pre–adult lives. Maybe it's a word on loneliness that you need. You sure can get to feeling alone when your time is consumed with little people who demand so much of you and don't allow you much time with others.

No matter what issue you are dealing with or question you search for an answer to, you can find a wealth of knowledge and guidance in My Word. Go ahead, look it up. Then soak it up and live it up. It will bless you beyond what you can imagine right now. I promise.

Lord, show me today in Your Word what I need to work through the issues of my day. I need You. I need Your truth. Amen.

BEYOND ME

"For as the sky soars high above earth, so the way I work surpasses the way you work, and the way I think is beyond the way you think."
Isaiah 55:9 msg

When young children can't wait for the next trip to shop for a hard-earned toy and then a favorite kids' meal for lunch, they have little idea how they might get themselves there. Even if they could find their way, they wouldn't know how to actually get the things they wanted. They are totally dependent on you to find the way, to get them from the vehicle to the building, to facilitate ordering and the exchange of money, or even to have money.

Now you've got a small picture of how My work and the way I think are not something you can comprehend. The good news is that you can depend on Me to get you where you're going. You know I'm watching over your every move, and I'm going to provide for you.

You already realize that this is often not going to look anything like what you may have envisioned. Don't be alarmed. Take the attitude of your child awaiting the shopping and lunch trip. Know that it's going to be great and that I'm going to get you there. That's all you need to know.

Lord, I put my trust in You today. Do the steering and protecting; You know exactly what I need. Amen.

ZOOMING OUT ON LIFE

From my distress I called upon the LORD; the LORD
answered me and set me in a large place.
PSALM 118:5 NASB

Feel penned in with the kids sometimes? Trapped by their schedules, incessant needs, and constant discipline? And even though your little ones aren't intentionally out to get you, it can feel that way!

In all your tight spaces, whether it's your children or others who are exhausting, you can run free in Me. I'll give you room to breathe that you didn't know existed. Peace beyond comprehension. Strength not humanly possible. Patience that is supernatural. I'm not saying it will all be a walk in the park. But I will give you wide-open meadows just beyond the thick, dark-woods moments.

The more you can pull back in your mind and look at the bigger picture from way beyond the treetops, the more accurate perspective you'll have. Suddenly your situations will not seem as big as they once did, and life will be more manageable.

Father, give me a view from a few thousand feet
so that I can get a better idea of how big Your
beautiful plan for my life really is. Amen.

CHRIST'S PRAYER FOR THOSE IN HIS CARE

*"I do not ask on behalf of these alone, but for those also who
believe in Me through their word; that they may all be one;
even as You, Father, are in Me and I in You, that they also may
be in Us, so that the world may believe that You sent Me."*
JOHN 17:20–21 NASB

The way I prayed for My disciples, these are the things that you want for your children, too.

You long for them to get along together. You protect them and pray for their protection beyond your presence. You hope more than anything that they will know My love, truth, and grace, as you do. You pray with everything you have that they will know Us (My Father, the Holy Spirit, and Me). That their lives will one day be led by Me outside of your care.

Oh, how I understand your longing for all of these things and more for your dear children. I still pray them for all My children—Our children, actually! So you keep praying, too—I'm listening.

*Lord God, I lay my children before You today.
Work on their behalf, in their hearts and minds.
Do the great work that only You can. Amen.*

BEAUTIFUL HOLY SPIRIT

"But I tell you the truth, it is to your advantage that I go away;
for if I do not go away, the Helper will not come to you; but if I go,
I will send Him to you. And He, when He comes, will convict
the world concerning sin and righteousness and judgment;
concerning sin, because they do not believe in Me."

JOHN 16:7–9 NASB

Those who walked the earth with Me were baffled by My leaving them. It took awhile for them to understand.

But ever since I sent the Holy Spirit, there has been greater faith among people. He gives conviction where it is needed, not guilt—don't confuse those two! He provides awareness of spiritual things. He speaks to hearts and enlightens minds with truth. He gives understanding of who I Am and why I came to save them. He is always in line with My Word. He helps people see with the eyes of their soul in ways that no human can communicate. He gives comfort, inspiration, and just the right motivation—right on time.

Lord, send Your Spirit today in powerful ways for me and my children,
that we would know You deeply and shine for You more brightly. Amen.

SWEET SCENTS OF FAITH

In the Messiah, in Christ, God leads us from place to place in one
perpetual victory parade. Through us, he brings knowledge of Christ.
Everywhere we go, people breathe in the exquisite fragrance.
2 CORINTHIANS 2:14 MSG

D irty laundry after a rainy soccer game, a pileup in the diaper bin, and
the bathroom during potty training—yikes! This motherhood parade
doesn't always smell so exquisite, does it?

On the contrary, though, your faithfulness and your faith itself are an
exquisite aroma to Me and those around you!

In Me and through the Holy Spirit, you go forward in this journey
of yours with beauty that draws others to Me. Even when you're going
through a tough time, when you let Me be your strength, others take notice.
When you are put to the test and come through strong, this is not lost on
those wondering about Me. They see it. Most of all, your children see it.

Father God, one step at a time today, help me
to walk in You, emanating Your
goodness in my life. Amen.

OUTRAGEOUS LOVE

The amazing grace of the Master, Jesus Christ,
the extravagant love of God, the intimate
friendship of the Holy Spirit, be with all of you.
2 CORINTHIANS 13:14 MSG

A best girlfriend is a joy to spend time with. You laugh together, encourage one another, and help each other in beautiful ways. She knows you well and can step in at times when others wouldn't know how to begin. A good friend knows how to comfort you, how to help you, and how to love you.

As wonderful and satisfying as a great friendship is, even more so is Our love for you. It's truly incomprehensible how much We love you. Truly. It would blow your mind! And We're with you always, hearing your every prayer and watching your back (and every direction, actually). This love is so rich and full—well, there are not enough pages to contain its expression.

How I love to watch you love and care for your children, how you are My arms and legs in so many ways.

How I love you, dear, sweet woman. I love you!

Precious Mighty God, go with me today in power
and strength unique to only You. How I need You in
my work as a mother, today and every day. Amen.

Shelley R. Lee has authored numerous articles and three books, contributing to many others; most recently, May's devotions in the 2015 Daily Wisdom for Women Collection (Barbour). Her bachelor's degree in communications came from Grand Valley State University in Michigan, where she met her husband of twenty-nine years, David. They've had the joy of being parents to one daughter who went on to eternity early, and four twenty-something sons whose humor and adventure keep them on their toes. Residing in northwest Ohio, Shelley is enjoying a daughter-in-law these days and happily awaits the arrival of her first grandchild.